AUSTRALIA

Go Exploring! Continents and Oceans

By Steffi Cavell-Clarke

©This edition was published in 2018. First published in 2017.

Book Life
King's Lynn
Norfolk PE30 4LS

ISBN: 978-1-78637-057-0

All rights reserved
Printed in Malaysia

Written by:
Steffi Cavell-Clarke

Edited by:
Grace Jones

Designed by:
Natalie Carr

A catalogue record for this book is available from the British Library.

All facts, statistics, web addresses and URLs in this book were verified as valid and accurate at time of writing. No responsibility for any changes to external websites or references can be accepted by either the author or publisher.

AUSTRALIA

CONTENTS

Words in **red** can be found in the glossary on page 23.

WHAT IS A CONTINENT?

A continent is a very large area of land that covers part of the Earth's surface. There are seven continents in total. There are also five oceans that surround the seven continents.

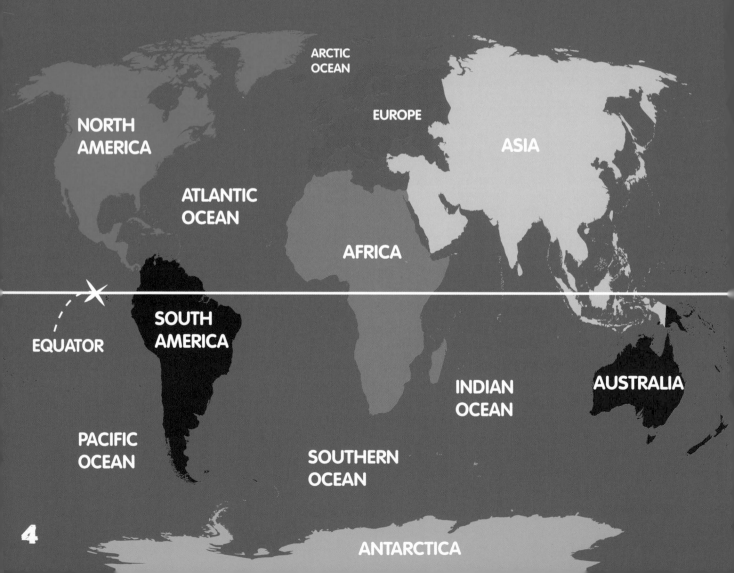

ARCTIC OCEAN

EUROPE

ASIA

NORTH AMERICA

ATLANTIC OCEAN

AFRICA

SOUTH AMERICA

EQUATOR

INDIAN OCEAN

AUSTRALIA

PACIFIC OCEAN

SOUTHERN OCEAN

ANTARCTICA

The seven continents are home to the Earth's **population.** Each continent has many different types of weather, landscape and wildlife. Let's go exploring!

WHERE IS AUSTRALIA?

Australia is the smallest continent in the world. It is **located** to the south of Asia and to the north of Antarctica. The Australian continent is completely surrounded by the Pacific and Indian Oceans.

Perth, Australia

Pacific Ocean

Australia

Indian Ocean

N
W   E
S

The Australian continent mainly covers a large country also called Australia. It includes a few **islands** around the mainland, such as Tasmania and Papua New Guinea. This area is also known as **Oceania**.

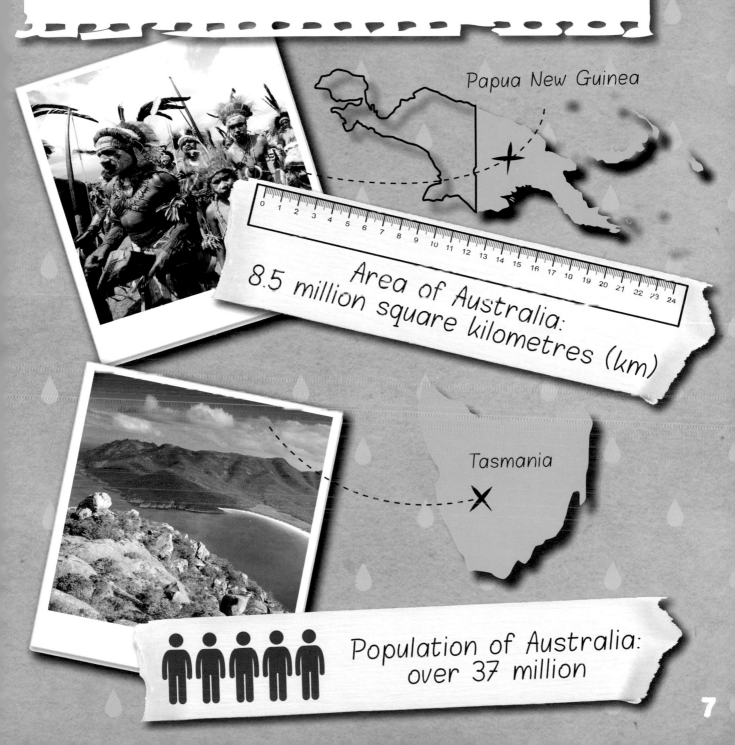

Papua New Guinea

Area of Australia: 8.5 million square kilometres (km)

Tasmania

Population of Australia: over 37 million

OCEANS

A sea is an extremely large area of salt water. The biggest seas in the world are called oceans. Just like countries, seas and oceans have different names.

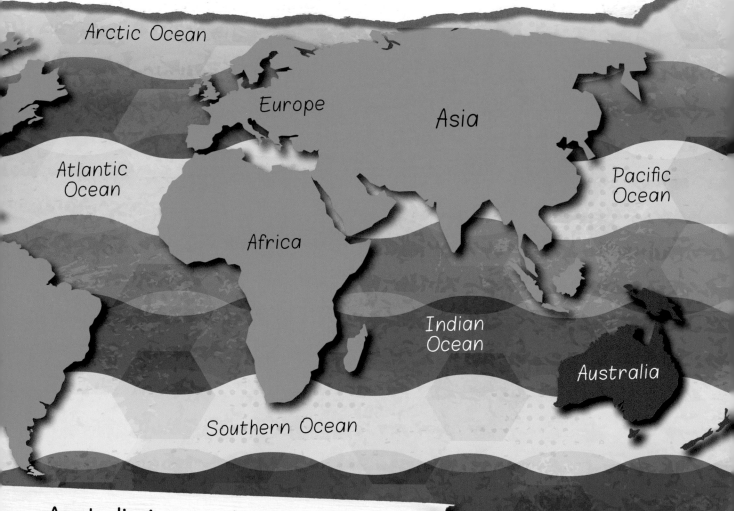

Arctic Ocean

Europe

Asia

Atlantic Ocean

Pacific Ocean

Africa

Indian Ocean

Australia

Southern Ocean

Australia is completely surrounded by the Pacific and Indian Oceans.

FACT FILE

Pacific Ocean
Area: 32% of Earth's surface
Average Depth: 4,280 metres

Indian Ocean
Area: 20% of Earth's surface
Average Depth: 3,890 metres

Depth is how deep the water is.

Pacific Ocean

Indian Ocean

COUNTRIES

The Australian continent is mostly made up of one country, Australia. It also includes other islands such as Papa New Guinea and Tasmania.

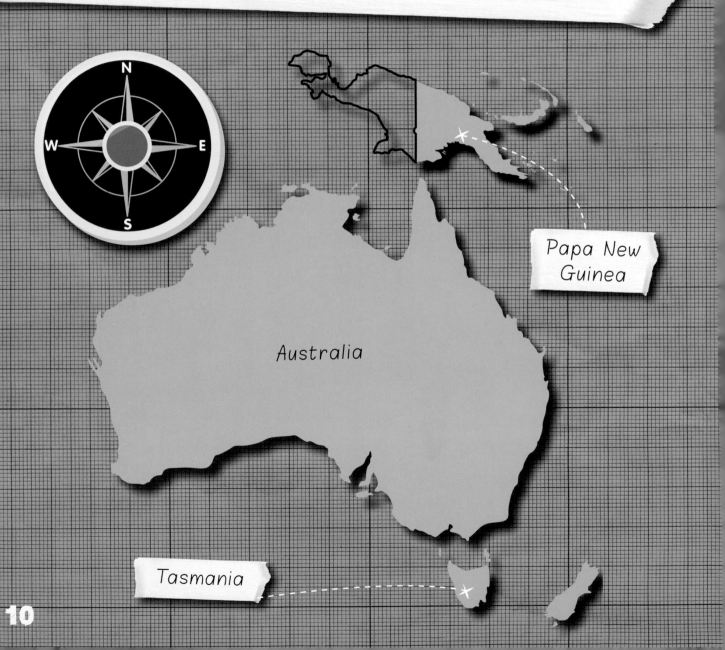

Papa New Guinea

Australia

Tasmania

FACT FILE

Largest Country	Australia	7.69 million square kilometres
Most Populated City	Sydney, Australia	Over 4.6 million
Famous Landmark	Great Barrier Reef, Australia	2,300 kilometres long
Highest Peak	Mount Kosciuszko, Australia	4,884 metres high
Dangerous Animal	Box jellyfish	Lives in Pacific Ocean

WEATHER

The Australian continent lies just south of the **Equator**. The Equator runs along the middle of the Earth, which is the warmest part of the world. Australia is so large, the **climate** changes across the continent.

Colder

Hotter

Equator

Hotter

Colder

Australia

The north of Australia has a **tropical** climate because it is closer to the equator. Central Australia has a very hot and dry climate with very little rainfall. The climate becomes cooler towards the south.

Tropical Climate

Hot & Dry Climate

Cooler Climate

North

South

Central

LANDSCAPE

There are many different types of landscape across the Australian continent. There are tropical rainforests, hot deserts and cool **coastal** areas.

Most of Australia's land is flat, dry desert. Around 35% of Australia's land is desert as it receives very little rainfall throughout the year.

The Great Victoria Desert is the largest desert on the Australian continent. In the day, the temperatures are extremely hot, but in the night, temperatures can be freezing.

Great Victoria Desert

Large desert areas are also known as the Outback.

Australia is famous for the Great Barrier Reef, which stretches for 2,300 kilometres along its north-eastern coastline.It lies in the Coral Sea which has warm, clear waters. It is home to many bright and colourful corals and fish.

Great Barrier Reef

Australia

The Pacific Ocean is the largest and deepest ocean in the world. There are many islands in the Pacific Ocean around the mainland of Australia. Some of these islands have a high, **mountainous** landscape, while others are very small or flat.

WILDLIFE

Australia is home to many types of animal. Wildlife can be found all over the continent and its surrounding islands.

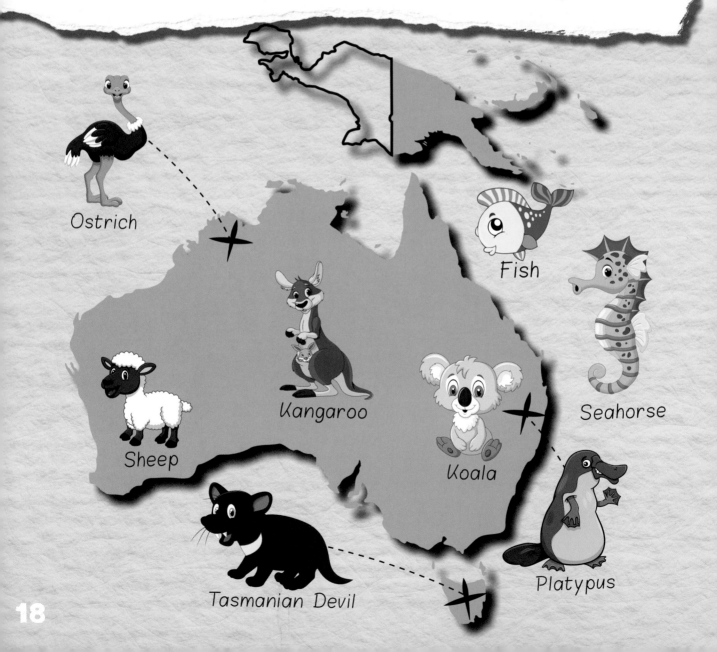

Ostrich

Fish

Seahorse

Kangaroo

Sheep

Koala

Tasmanian Devil

Platypus

Pouch

Baby Kangaroo

A kangaroo can cover over 8 metres of land in a single jump!

Kangaroos are **native** to Australia. They mostly live on the dry **plains** of Australia and Papua New Guinea. They can grow up to 1.5 metres tall and eat plants. The kangaroo carries its baby in a pouch on the front of its body.

SETTLEMENTS

The country of Australia has been split into six areas called states. New South Wales has the highest population with over 7.5 million people living in it. Most people live in big cities such as Sydney or Melbourne.

Northern Territory

Queensland

Western Australia

South Australia

New South Wales

Victoria

Sydney

Melbourne

Many people who live on the surrounding islands live in towns or small farming villages. The farmers often grow crops such as sugar cane and corn.

Sugar Cane Plant

Cornfield

THE ENVIRONMENT

The world's temperature is rising; this is called **global warming**. As the temperature rises, the oceans will become warmer. This change in temperature can harm sea life, such as that found on the Great Barrier Reef.

Great Barrier Reef

Melting Ice Caps

To protect the oceans, we must all take care of the environment.

GLOSSARY

climate the average weather of an area

coastal near to a sea

equator imaginary line running around the middle of the earth

global warming the slow rise of the earth temperature

islands areas of land surrounded by water

located where something can be found

mountainous an area of land that has many mountains

native common to a particular place

Oceania the name of a large area that covers part of the Pacific Ocean and its islands

plains large areas of flat land with few trees

population number of people living in a place

tropical warm and wet areas near the equator

INDEX

PHOTOCREDITS

Abbreviations: l–left, r–right, b–bottom, t–top, c–centre, m–middle.

Front Cover Background – Flas100. Front cover vectors – elenabsl. 2t – stockphoto–graf. 2tr – Kletr. 2br – Martin Valigursky. 3tr – structuresxx. 3br – Visun Khankasem. 4tl – elenabsl. 5tl – Visun Khankasem. 5tm - structuresxx. 5tr – structuresxx. 5bl - Brian Kinney. 5br – robert cicchetti. 6&7 background – Irtsya. 6ml – Marcella Miriello. 7tl – isaxar. 7bl – Totajla. 8 background – gudinny. 9 vectors – yyang. 9bl – ana_sky. 9m – 89studio. 9 background – taviphoto. 10 background - Taigi. 11 background – schab. 11m – PILart. 11tr – Aleksey Klints. 12 background – Igor Kovalchuk. 12ml – Johan Swanepoel. 12br – Aleksandar Todorovic. 13tr – CristinaMuraca. 13br – structuresxx. 13bl – ChameleonsEye. 13 background – Markovka. 14&15 background – Kaesler Media. 14ml – AustralianCamera. 14mr – Renata Apanaviciene. 15mtl – pisaphotography. 15mbl – structuresxx. 16tl – deb22. 16tr – Brian Kinney. 16mb – Brian Kinney. 16ml – Kletr. 16br – Pantera. 17 background – Anna Poguliaeva. 17t – Tanya Puntti. 17m – Regien Paassen. 18 vectors – Klara Viskova, Teguh Mujiono, Muhammad Desta Laksana, Igor Zakowski, Pushkin, Memo Angeles. 19 background – yoshi0511. 19m – structuresxx. 20 background – gudinny. 20mr – Taras Vyshnya. 20br – Aleksandar Todorovic. 21 background – sash77. 21br – Vaclav Volrab. 21l – Hywit Dimyadi. 22ml – Brian Kinney. 22mr – TrashTheLens. Images are courtesy of Shutterstock.com. With thanks to Getty Images, Thinkstock Photo and iStockphoto.